Poems
to Make You Laugh

Poems to Make You Laugh

Flossie Hatfield Smith

VANTAGE PRESS
New York / Los Angeles / Chicago

FIRST EDITION

All rights reserved, including the right of
reproduction in whole or in part in any form.

Copyright © 1989 by Flossie Hatfield Smith

Published by Vantage Press, Inc.
516 West 34th Street, New York, New York 10001

Manufactured in the United States of America
ISBN: 0-533-08572-1

Library of Congress Catalog Card No.: 89-90191

To those who encouraged me and those who inspired me

CONTENTS

Introduction 1
The Faultfinder 2
The Dignified Attorney 3
The Backbiter 4
The Non-Flyer 5
The Undertaker 6
The Lush 9
The Registered Nurse 11
"I Know Too Much" 14
The Distraught Widower 15
Stingy 17
#1 Landlord 20
The Wife Beater 23
The Ambitious Youth 25
The Fools Walk Inn 27
My Friend, Lee 29
Mirror, Mirror on the Wall 31
Freeloader's Christmas Eve 33
The Dedicated Teacher 35
A Peaceful School Day 37
Hyper Tam 40
A Tearful Retirement 42
The Carnival 45
A Ship of Fools 48
Time for School To End 51
First Grade Student 53
The Preacher's Wife 55
The Hairdresser 57

The Secretary	59
The Widow	61
The Doctor	63
Ms. Tongue	65
Watch—You May Get What You Pray For	66
My Meandering Love Life	68
Love Conquers All???	69
The Other Woman	71
On a Check	73
Poor People Have Poor Ways	75
My Will	77
TV Preacher	79

Poems
to Make You Laugh

INTRODUCTION

Take no offense to my poems.
They are written for fun.
Before you read long, though,
You will picture someone.

But just keep on reading,
And before you are through,
It's most likely you'll read one
That reminds you of you.

Names in my poems
Are fictitious, too.
Don't be mad if you find one
With the same name as you.

THE FAULTFINDER

I vow to always keep a frown
And look for someone to run down.
No situation can exist
That I can't give an ugly twist.

If I see someone who is glad,
I'll find a way to make him sad.
I punch and probe—I stab and pick.
That is how I get my kicks.

I scowl all day—I frown all night.
I find what's wrong and hide what's right.
Good deeds you may ever do,
But I'll make them look bad on you.

I find fault with everything.
I'd find a flaw in an angel's wing.
I don't know why the world can't see
That all are out of line but me.

I'll bring gloom to anyone.
I'd cover up the brightest sun.
I want everyone to be
Sour and miserable just like me.

I hope someday to find my way
Up to the pearly gates,
But I'll lay odds of ten to one
The pearls are not in straight.

THE DIGNIFIED ATTORNEY

I am a dignified attorney.
Fool with me, and I will burn ye.
I'm trained so well at being nice,
I'll wrap you 'round my finger twice.

You'll think that I'm your dearest friend,
That I'll stick with you till the end—
On my shoulder you may lean
While your pockets I do clean.

You'd best enjoy your property.
Soon it will belong to me.
When your spouse is titled, "late,"
I'll con you out of your estate.

Divorces are my specialty.
I tear up lives, then laugh with glee.
I throw the fat right in the flame,
Then rob a man and ruin his name.

I bleed him till he's whipped and broke.
Soon his future's just a joke.
No situation will stop me.
I have no use for decency.

I'll surely get your black lung through—
Four-fifths for me, one-fifth for you.
Thanks for crawling in the mine
To buy my Cadillac so fine.

I enter in my daily log
The many ways to be a hog.
I'll live it up—I'll have my say;
I'm bound for torment anyway.

THE BACKBITER

You've bit my back down to my slacks.
You've really done me in.
Don't ask me why—I do not know,
But maybe you will win.

You find such joy in hurting me
And making me seem small.
But yet you smile and speak to me
And try to fake it all.

You go to church and testify
And saintly seem to be—
But he who kicks his brother
Is a hypocrite to me.

Just keep punching everyday.
You're sure to get what's due.
There was a place for Judas,
And there'll be a place for you.

THE NON-FLYER

I got your ticket, but no thanks.
In my opinion, flying "stanks."
The thought of flying makes me ill.
I haven't flown and never will.

I'd like very much to visit you.
I'd like to see the ocean blue,
But you'll just have to realize
I will not fly the friendly skies.

Statistics do not mean a thing.
I just don't trust a man-made wing.
Don't mention flying or I panic.
I'd feel as safe on the *Titanic*.

I'll get a train or catch a boat;
I'd even ride a billy goat,
But don't expect me to report.
I will not be at the airport.

I will not fly—I will not soar.
I'll stay on land forever more.
Never will I board a plane
Unless I am pronounced insane.

THE UNDERTAKER

Of all occupations, there are a few things worse
Than doing embalming and driving a hearse.
A big mistake you're likely to make,
If you decide to undertake.

From the time you are called a pick-up to make,
You go like a streak, till your whole body aches.
Your patient is quiet, but you really strive
To satisfy those that are left alive.

Getting obituary information
Is not always easy in this occupation.
Sometimes you get such an offbeat reply
That you don't know whether to laugh or cry.

Once I was asking a lady questions,
Trying to get the right information.
"Is the spouse deceased?" I asked, and she said,
"No, Undertaker, her husband is dead."

After the arrangements have been called in,
They change plans and want it published again.
A relative calls and screams at you—
You failed to mention his great uncle Lou.

Spectators come early to the wake,
So they can watch and see the heartache.
Some come in bent over with grief,
While others don't try to hide their relief.

The first thing you can expect to be said,
Is "Why does Poppy look like he's dead?"
They'll find many things that are wrong,
Like, "His hair is too thin," and "His nose is too long."

The sitting rooms are soon filled with smoke.
Some laugh, others cry, and some tell dirty jokes.
There are usually some there with bloodshot eyes,
Who've been hitting the bottle, you realize.

People bring children of every kind.
They plunder in everything they can find.
They continually run to the bathroom sink
To see how much water they can drink.

When things simmer down and the wake's under way,
And you think things are going to be okay,
You hear a loud scream—how much more can you stand?
Some kid's closed the casket lid on his hand.

You shake in your boots and pretend to be calm,
Thinking, "Why did I ever want to embalm?"
Proud of yourself you'll surely be,
If you can hang on to your sanity.

Finally it's over, and the last person goes,
Two hours later than you're scheduled to close.
It's time to clean ash trays and get paper cups.
The restrooms look like they've been used by pups.

When you get to sleep, the phone breaks your slumber—
Someone forgot to give you his unlisted number.
Long before daylight, there's a knock at your door—
A friend couldn't make it the night before.

Ere the funeral begins, you're in for a treat—
Outsiders have taken the family seats.
You don't dare make a single soul mad.
The next body you get may be him or his dad.

Your telephone rings—your doorbell sounds,
As pressure grows by leaps and bounds.
When the services are ready to start,
You're wishing it was over with all your heart.

When the viewing begins, don't be alarmed,
If a three hundred pounder faints in your arms.
You wonder how much your frame can take,
Before your ribs begin to break.

When, at last, you're loaded to depart,
You turn on the keys, and the hearse won't start.
You charge the battery, to get it to go,
As you feel your hair turn as white as snow.

You finally get through it without passing out,
So relieved that it's over, you almost shout.
By the time it's all finished and everyone's gone,
You feel a great deal like the funeral's your own.

Now if you've decided that your life's ambition
Is to fulfill the duties of a mortician,
Do well and word will soon get around,
That you'll be the last to let a friend down.

THE LUSH

I'm a lush. I am a boozer.
I'm what you call a self-willed loser.
I fill myself with wine and beer,
Then I get out and show my rear.

I drink until I sway and reel,
Then plant myself behind a wheel.
I drive my car from side to side,
While other drivers duck and hide.

When I decide to pitch a drunk
I say I have the flu,
Then go I quickly to the store
To get my jug of brew.

I soon am loaded to the brim.
My senses then get numb.
I scatter trash and make a mess
And look just like a bum.

I cannot go to work, of course.
My drinking takes first place.
I lay my whole life on the line.
Tomorrow I won't face.

I stand to lose my license,
Then I can't drive a car.
I stand to lose my income
All for my moonshine jar.

I skimp on food. I skimp on heat.
I'll drink although I may not eat.
I do not have enough to wear.
My 'phone's gone now, but I don't care.

I have not found myself a wife.
I choose to lead a lonely life.
I'll drink up all I'll ever own.
I am a win-o to the bone.

The boat has left me long ago.
I was too drunk to see it go.
It sailed off on a sea of wine,
While I messed up this life of mine.

THE REGISTERED NURSE

If you've decided to be a nurse,
Maybe you'd like to talk to me first.
I've worked two years as a full time R.N.,
So to you who are outside looking in:

I've had time to learn what it's all about,
And it's different from the inside looking out.
I took classes needed to graduate,
Then took the test required by the state.

Man, what a test! I'll tell you now,
I passed it, but I don't know how.
Next I began looking for a position
Working as a nurse beside a physician.

I thought a job would be easy to find,
But I was soon to change my mind.
I was interviewed by Dr. Zeke.
He asked me if I liked to streak.

I said I wasn't trained for streaking.
No job from Zeke—I still was seeking.
A hospital finally gave to me
A job that began my shift at three.

I wished I could have worked by day,
But knew I couldn't have my way.
I went to work all dressed in white,
Hoping to have a quiet night.

I found out that it wouldn't be.
A light was soon turned on for me.
About that time I heard a bell,
Turned to run, but slipped and fell.

I picked me up and ran to see
Why my patient rang for me.
He wanted me to feel his head,
And asked me if his face was red.

Soon I was running, to and fro.
A light said stop—a bell said go.
One patient laughed, another swore.
Push, run, and lift forevermore!

I have to check on Mr. Strong,
Who says he cannot be here long.
He's not as sick as you may think.
He's pert enough to pinch and wink.

I have to rush to Mrs. Plott
To give another water shot
And help her make believe she's sick.
She really needs a good hard kick.

I've learned to watch for nurse abuse,
—To dodge loose cups and flying shoes.
I'll surely watch the next O.B.
The last one took a bite of me.

Clean, scrub, and sterilize!
Bedpans galore to sanitize.
I've cleaned till I am in a spin.
I'll tape that pan to Bedpan Ben.

I've run until my legs are sore,
But still I've got to run some more.
I'll have to check on Mr. Lee,
Who stays wound up in his IV.

That win-o down in 103
Keeps turning on his light for me.
He says if I don't give him wine,
He'll black these two brown eyes of mine.

There sits a tank of oxygen
As lethal as a loaded gun.
If I don't watch Nicotine Joe,
He'll strike a match and we'll all blow.

Things start out bad and then get worse.
That's how it goes with a registered nurse.
There's first one problem, then another.
I think I'll go back home to Mother.

If nursing is still what you want to do,
I'll shake your hand. Hooray for you!
Do your work well. Do not fail.
Don't disappoint Florence Nightingale.

"I KNOW TOO MUCH"

I'm a big black dog—my name is Dutch.
I have a problem—I know too much.
I wander around in the neighborhood,
And see much that's bad and little that's good.

The man next door has kicked his wife,
Slapped her face, and threatened her life.
The kids hide out until he's gone.
—Even the flies leave this man alone.

Mrs. LaLee is a neighbor of mine.
She keeps a supply of whiskey and wine.
A red light from her window does glow.
She's a very busy woman, as men come and go.

While Mary Bell was in the hospital ill,
John Bell had a guest—his secretary, Lill.
When Mary came home, feeling some better,
It made me sick to see John and Lill pet her.

Down the street two doors are two mean boys.
They've stolen all the other kids' toys.
They paint and redo them and call them their own.
If the kids come to get them, they hit them with stones.

Mr. Hall is the mayor of our town.
He sells drugs to kids, when the sun goes down.
It makes my blood boil when I hear the remark:
"You're as low as a dog—I expect you to bark."

If you must call me something bad,
Call me a snake or a fat crawdad.
Don't *ever, ever* call me a man,
Or I'll bite a piece out of you, if I can!

THE DISTRAUGHT WIDOWER

Janie was a loving wife.
"Jim, darling," seemed to be her life.
She cooked his very favorite dishes
And lived to satisfy his wishes.

Their house was clean and smoothly run.
She stayed up nights to get things done.
Jim's clothes were always clean and pressed.
At church he looked his very best.

Janie went to work each day.
The bills were hard for Jim to pay.
She bought him everything she could.
For Jimmy, nothing was too good.

She carried an insurance policy
To give him some security,
In case he should be left behind,
Perhaps some comfort he would find.

She gave their children lots of love,
But darling Jim was held above
All things. She always made it clear
He was the thing she held most dear.

Too swiftly Janie's life did fly.
Her time was up—she said good-bye.
Jim said his life was torn apart.
No one could heal his broken heart.

People showed such deep concern.
So many things he'd need to learn.
They dreaded loneliness he faced.
Janie could not be replaced.

Jim promptly settled Jane's estate.
She'd left all to her darling mate.
He cashed in everything she had.
Jim darling didn't do too bad.

The neighbors watched him with surprise.
Some could not believe their eyes.
He soon was spending Janie's money
On a bleached out blonde called Bunny.

Jim bought himself a curly wig.
He learned to do the mating jig.
He said his car was much too tiny
And bought a Lincoln, long and shiny.

He put his church clothes all away
And bought some for the modern day.
T-shirts and sandals took their place
To match his smiling macho face.

He hits the road each night at dark
To find his blonde and park and spark.
Jim lives a swinging marathon.
He prowls all night till early dawn.

Here's food for thought, you trusting wives.
You might as well enjoy your lives.
Don't sacrifice for that spouse—
Chances are, you've married a louse.

Don't skimp and save for any man.
Spend it, lend it, while you can.
He won't despair. His heart won't break.
He'll find a new love at your wake.

STINGY

I doubt if you will ever see
Anyone half as stingy as me.
I don't think you will ever know
Another who loves money so.

I built myself a four-room house
Upon a little hill,
But found out that it cost too much
To pay the power bill.

I soon thought of a simple plan
To bring expenses down.
I simply had two rooms torn off.
The answer I have found.

In wintertime my house is cool.
I do not wish to waste my fuel.
I do not sit up late at night,
So I won't have to burn a light.

In summertime my house gets hot.
I really need a fan,
But I can't let the money go.
I'll stand it if I can.

My furniture is all worn out,
But I will not replace it.
I lean it up against the wall,
With rocks and sticks to brace it.

My kitchenwares are chipped and bent,
But beauty does not count.
My old ones feed me just as well.
They hold the same amount.

I had a dog—I named him Moe.
He ate so much I let him go.
He ate first one thing, then another,
Till I gave him to my step-brother,

My clothes are worn and out of style.
I wear them for a long, long while.
This apparel suits me fine.
Nobody else has clothes like mine.

At church they pass the plate to me.
I don't know what they think.
I put a nickel in one time,
Then could not sleep a wink.

I do not go to beauty shops.
Their prices I won't pay.
My brother cuts my hair for free.
That's why I look this way.

I have no problem with my weight.
I don't buy costly food.
I fast till I am almost starved,
Then anything tastes good.

My teeth began to ache and throb me.
I would not let the dentists rob me.
I found one who did cheap extractions
And put my bare gums into action.

Eye doctors' prices are too much,
But they'll cheat me no more.
I get my reading glasses
At the ten-cent store.

I hope some day to go up to
The land of milk and honey,
But won't be satisfied unless
They let me take my money.

1 LANDLORD

When Grandpa left to me some land,
I felt a fortune in my hand.
A wealthy landlord I would be—
I had myself a money tree.

I build a condo, nice and neat,
Decked out for the most elite.
Kind and generous I would be,
—Not full of greed, like Simon Legree.

If I treated tenants well,
Perfect conditions would prevail.
Soon my place was rented out.
I was so happy, I could shout.

Right off, I got a late night call—
Someone's neighbor was having a ball.
I went to see what I could do,
And had to dodge a flying shoe.

It was dawn, ere things were quiet.
I went home shaky and very uptight.
There wasn't a day without some trouble.
Renters were beginning to burst my bubble.

I rented to dignified Mr. Hood.
He'd act right, if anyone would.
He soon was delinquent with his rent.
I went to check and smelled a scent.

Of whiskey, mixed with beer and ale.
His eyes were glassy—his face was pale.
He moved out, owing me some cash,
Leaving his apartment full of trash.

Next to rent were Carl and Jean—
Young, modern, very clean.
I almost lost my tonsils when
They rolled their motorcycle in.

Soon the cops were on the scene.
They caught and captured Carl and Jean.
The bike was stolen, naturally.
The thought had not occurred to me.

Carl had escaped from the state pen.
I'd used poor judgement, once again.
Carl and Jean were on the run.
Both were armed with knives and guns.

One rainy night at half past three,
A lady called and ordered me
To fix a leaking roof right then.
My patience sure was growing thin.

Rain was dripping on her bed—
I'd fix it or she'd crack my head.
Another lady, very tight,
Turned her heaters off at night.

The water froze to solid ice.
She didn't do it once, but twice.
A man got shocked—there was a short.
Of course, he took me straight to court.

He charged me with count after count.
I had to pay a huge amount.
A couple took a week-long trip—
They didn't let the water drip,

But left it running open wide.
The pump burned up—I could have cried.
I watch sorry renters come and go,
And grow more tired of eating crow.

I see that renting is the pits.
I wish that place would blow to bits!
Move on over, Simon Legree—
You have a lot more sense than me.

THE WIFE BEATER

When I can't take the stress of life,
I take my spite out on my wife.
When worldly problems get to me,
I give my wife some hickory tea.

She wears her makeup thick and dark,
To cover up the telltale marks.
Sunglasses hide her sore, black eyes.
She looks like someone in disguise.

A man at work gave me a cheating.
I thought, "I'll give my wife a beating."
I went storming in the house,
To try my fists out on my spouse.

I hit one lick and I did see
My beloved swing at me.
I felt a pain across my lip,
And then another on my hip.

Something ripped right down my thigh,
Then bright, red blood began to fly.
I didn't know my darling wife
Was holding in her fist, a knife.

I passed out, cold, upon the floor.
Soon I was carried out the door.
They took me to emergency,
Where a surgeon worked on me.

Now I am lying here in bed;
My leg is raised above my head.
I'll bet I have two hundred stitches.
I cannot wear a shirt or britches.

When stressful problems get me down,
I will not knock my wife around.
I never dreamed the little wife
Could be so handy with a knife.

THE AMBITIOUS YOUTH

I have a mind all my own.
My head is hard, like a stone.
I know what is best for me.
I know it all, from A to Z.

I am young—I am free.
And my life belongs to me.
I have the key to unlock all.
Into my life no rain will fall.

An education I don't need.
I quit school to smoke the weed.
I know more than teachers do.
I'll win most and lose very few.

I do not need to get a job
As long as I can steal and rob.
The future I do not forsee.
Time will not catch up with me.

Don't tell me how to drive a car.
My motto is, "Go fast! Go far!"
I'll sniff my coke and roll my tires.
I'll space out higher than the stars.

Don't tell me how I should dress.
I'll grow a beard to my chest.
I'll wear my hair long and oiled.
I'll wear my clothes tight and soiled.

Years have passed. I've changed my mood.
I've also changed my attitude.
I live a life all my own
In a house made of stone.

In grayish stripes I am dressed.
I wear a number on my chest.
I no longer reach the stars,
Since I am peeping through the bars.

THE FOOLS WALK INN

My parents were strict and a little strait-laced.
They tried to prepare me for the life I faced.
My mother said I would have to decide
On the narrow road or the road that was wide.

Down the road, just around the bend
Was a swinging joint called "The Fools Walk Inn."
I'd been warned since I was a tiny lad
To stay away from that place—it was nothing but bad.

I'd been told of the gash on Uncle Joe's jaw
And the scar on Uncle Ed's chin.
They got those marks on a Saturday night
In a fight at Fools Walk Inn.

When I was sixteen I decided to go
Where things were swinging—I'd go with the flow.
I dressed myself as neat as a pin,
And headed straight for The Fools Walk Inn.

I opened the door and said, "Howdy, all!"
Things got so quiet you could hear a leaf fall.
I don't know when I've ever seen
So many guys so big and mean.

One guy stood up and said with a grunt,
"Why are you here, you puny runt?"
I said, "I just stopped by to visit."
He said, "It ain't visiting hours, is it?

"The last stranger that stopped by here
Left with only part of an ear."
"Let him have it!" someone said.
I felt a blow upon my head.

I tried to move toward the door,
But someone knocked me on the floor.
Another stepped upon my hip,
Then he slapped me on my lip.

I got upon my knees to crawl
And felt my body hit the wall.
One got a fistful of my hair—
Another threw me through the air.

I landed hard upon the ground.
I was too scared to make a sound.
I picked up what was left of me.
My head was spinning—I could hardly see.

My shins were bleeding—I'd lost my shoes.
My face was nothing but a bruise.
My eyes felt like two burning coals.
My arms felt like two broken poles.

I went limping back around the bend,
And said good-bye to The Fools Walk Inn.
I sneaked in the door, black, blue and red.
Mom looked at me and shook her head.

I was sick and sore for more than a week.
Now I listen when my elders speak.
When I have a son, I wonder if he
Will grow up to be as foolish as me.

MY FRIEND, LEE

I had a friend by name of Lee.
He was a guy who worked with me.
I was so glad to have someone
To talk to, when I was alone.

Lee's mother had been very ill.
He had to pay her doctor bills.
He had a hard time paying them—
I felt a deep concern for him.

I had a town house, rather large.
I moved Lee in, without a charge.
I shared my food—I did not mind,
For true blue friends are hard to find.

I paid for all our double dates,
Thankful to afford the rates.
In time I found myself a wife.
Lee shared our happy, married life.

Ruth said that it would be okay
If I asked my friend Lee to stay.
We treated him like royalty.
Nothing was too good for Lee.

Later on I came home, late.
I thought Lee was on a date,
For nobody was around.
I did not hear a single sound.

I checked our room and almost moaned.
Ruth's clothes and make-up were all gone.
Lee's belongings were gone, too.
—So was my auto, bright and new.

Then I knew the naked truth.
Lee had gone—he'd left with Ruth.
I knew that with a friend like Lee
I did not need an enemy.

MIRROR, MIRROR ON THE WALL

"Mirror, mirror on the wall,
I am not having fun at all.
I look into you, and I see
Better times ahead for me."

I know I do not look the same,
But I'm still full of fun and games.
I can't believe I've lost my touch.
I really haven't aged that much.

Although I am no longer young,
There are some songs I haven't sung.
There are some bells I need to ring.
I've not had time to do my thing.

I know my wife has been true blue,
But I deserve somebody new.
I'll stop in at the nearest bar
And find a young chick to admire.

I found that new love of my life.
I just forgot I had a wife,
But she soon learned of my affair,
And cleaned me out from here to there.

She said, "My love, you now are free,"
And put the rollers under me.
The judge has lowered the boom on me,
So I now live in poverty.

Since alimony I now pay,
My young chick has flown away.
She left me quicker than a flash,
As soon as I ran out of cash.

I think about my former life—
My pretty home, my kids, my wife.
It wasn't very bright of me
To try to change my destiny.

This is not the way I planned it.
I burned a blister. I must stand it.
"Mirror, mirror on the wall
You built me up, then let me fall."

FREELOADER'S CHRISTMAS EVE

On the night before Christmas, all through our house,
Not a critter was sober—not even a louse.
We had all hit the sack anywhere we could find.
In our polluted condition nothing troubled our minds.

Our biggest stockings we slung on a chair,
Hoping Old Santa would promptly be there.
I set out empty boxes and a big garbage can.
When it comes to freeloading, we get all we can.

Dad home from the still, and Mom, home from the bar,
Had just staggered in and stretched out by the fire,
When from the outside I heard such a noise,
I thought it must be the revenue boys.

I jumped up in a tizzy and ran into Pa's brew.
He yelled, "Watch it, son, or I'll break you in two!"
I ran to the window and what did I see?
Dear old Santa, as mad as could be.

"Move, Dasher and Prancer! Watch out for that tree!
I know it's no picnic, but you're no better than me.
Move Comet and Vixen, you dumb billy goats!
Shape up and get with it, or I'll slit your blamed throats!"

Within a few seconds I heard a loud crack,
So I knew he had made it to the top of our shack.
Santa fell down the chimney in a sooty cloud.
He picked himself up and cursed long and loud.

He looked all around and said, "Saints preserve me!
What this dump needs is some TNT."
He reached in the sack and pulled out a few things—
A car with three wheels and a plane without wings,

A cross-eyed doll and a crooked bat,
A silent whistle and a ball with a flat.
He grabbed two rotten apples and a loaf of stale bread,
Plus some dried up oranges and a cabbage head.

He pulled out a carton of out dated eggs
And a stuffed tomcat with only two legs.
"These things aren't so hot—I don't guess they will love 'em,
But for all I care, if they don't, they can shove 'em."

He ended the job with a smashed Christmas wreath,
And zoomed up the chimney gritting his teeth.
He jumped in his sleigh and yelled, "Clear out of here,
Before we're all drunk from smelling stale beer!

"If I call on more families that act this way
I'll junk this sleigh and get on D.P.A."
—And I heard him roar as he sped out of sight,
"Spit on you all! What a heck of a night!"

THE DEDICATED TEACHER

Do I like to teach school? The answer is, "No!"
Do you like to stand out in the hot sun and hoe
Or wash walls higher than you can reach?
That's how well I like to teach.

Why do I do it? There's just one hitch.
I didn't happen to be born rich.
I went to college and worked hard and long;
Now I teach school and work for a song.

I thought when I started to teach I would be
The boss in my classroom, as a teacher should be.
After all, I'd been trained to do my job well.
I felt I could handle anything that befell.

So I shined my good shoes, and dressed in my best,
And walked in my classroom feeling grand in my chest,
To discover a swarm of thirty and five
Wiggly first graders that were working alive.

My hopes soon were dashed—my confidence grew thin.
I felt like Daniel in the lion's den.
I hoped that the parents would help pull me through
By cooperating with a teacher so new.

They were good on one hand, but then on the other,
I had one that said, "Don't whip 'Little Brother.'
His nerves are bad and his heart can't take it.
Lift your hand at my boy and be sure I will break it.

"Another thing, be sure to remember,
There'll be an election in early November.
I'm always in good with the ones that run.
Don't touch 'Little Brother,' or your trouble's begun.

"I'll have you moved up a hollow so far,
You'll have to take sunshine with you in a jar."
With these words ringing clear, I started my day,
And soon learned how to earn all my pay.

"Little Brother" was ten and weighed ninety-two,
Was as strong as a bull and as mean as a shrew.
I learned to be kicked and bounce back like a ball.
I learned to be tough and prepared in the fall

To take what I had to, to stay on the staff
Of trained professionals. How's that for a laugh?
The years have gone by, and I've taught nearly thirty,
Without throwing things or talking too dirty.

With each year that's passed and brought on another,
I've always been blessed with a new "Little Brother,"
Who's left me with memories to do me for sure,
In spite of good children, I've had every year.

If you really think that teaching's for you,
Be ready to do what you don't want to.
Be ready to vote for the biggest crook
And forget all the training you ever took.

When I retire and make my speech,
If I tell you I like to teach,
Mash my mouth and black my eyes.
Kick me hard for telling lies.

A PEACEFUL SCHOOL DAY

Another school day—another fight.
Nelson can't read and Floyd can't write.
Pansy won't stay away from the door,
And Blaine doesn't know what a seat is for.

Jack doesn't know a T from an L.
Ellie can't count and Otis can't spell.
All Burl will do is sit and stare.
His body is here, but his mind is elsewhere.

I call a group up and get underway,
Trying my best to have a good day.
Rush whistles and hums—I ask him to stop.
Carl bursts a corn chip bag with a "pop!"

Saul comes in late with a scowl and a frown,
Looking for a small one he can knock down.
Lucite does nothing but tattle and tell,
From the time she arrives till the hometime bell.

Fern wants to be petted all the day.
She's sad because Daddy has gone away.
Joe has a problem, it's plain to see,
But because of his speech, he can't get through to me.

I get called to the office to take a 'phone call.
Garfield has lost his little green ball.
While I'm gone Lark turns over Shayde's chair,
And Zeke puts blow gum in Marybell's hair.

I'm determined to get some teaching done.
I motivate my class, and when we've begun,
Sue Ellen comes up as pale as a sheet,
And proceeds to up-chuck all over my feet.

Ray has spilled juice all over the floor.
At this time I hear a knock at the door.
Mrs. Darklight has stopped to complain.
LeeRoy has lost his jacket again.

I try to rewind and get going again,
When sleeping Don Arden comes dragging in.
I'll have to review him—he just takes what life gives,
And he'll be behind as long as he lives.

At the back of the room sits beady-eyed Mose,
Anxious to tell everything that he knows.
He knows obscene words that I've never heard,
But yet he can't read, not even a word.

The speaker comes on—I hear with dismay,
Reports were due day before yesterday.
I work hard at my job. I know how it's done,
But the odds are against me, fifteen to one.

By the end of the day my head is roaring,
My eyes are popping, and my blood pressure's soaring.
I'm glad the parking lot isn't far.
I hope I will recognize my car.

At last I get home and sit down to relax.
The telephone rings—it's Mr. Flax.
Arbutis came home two crayons short.
If I don't find them, he'll take me to court.

I hang up—the phone rings again.
Ms. Bark is as mad as a wet hen.
The bus has run without little Leck.
If he's gone ten more minutes, she'll break my neck.

Finally I get myself into bed,
With the day's events going 'round in my head.
I tuck myself in the turn off the light,
And pray I don't dream about school tonight.

HYPER TAM

I hear the door open and shut with a slam.
There's no doubt about it, here comes Hyper Tam.
He's much too excited to walk to his seat—
He turns two handsprings and lands on his feet.

He tosses his bookbag. The contents soar.
Pencils, crayons, and much, much, more.
He looks all around and gives a "Hoo-ray!"
I can see that my work is cut out for the day.

Next to the pencil sharpener he goes.
He makes sure he steps on Willis's toes.
He sharpens his pencil until it's all gone,
Bites off his eraser and spits it at Ron.

He attacks his writing with a scratch and a rake,
Finishes quickly and grabs little Jake.
I try to get order—his mood has caught wing.
The other kids all start doing their thing.

When it's time for reading, he runs like thunder
To grab a chair big enough to crawl under.
I pass the books out as fast as I can.
He tears out a page and makes him a fan.

Now it's time to do math and his workbooks are scattered.
The pages are already torn and tattered.
He's broken his crayons, his pencils are gone.
I find that I need all the patience I own.

As soon as my head turns he's down on the floor
Playing and fighting more and more.
Surely, today, if I don't miss my guess,
Little Tam will explode before last recess.

He makes it till playtime and goes out in a whirl,
Laughing and pulling at Sampson and Earl.
He comes back in, all covered with blood—
He's had a rock battle with Anderson Budd.

At hometime, he comes with a hug and a smile,
And asks, "Have I been good?" I say, "Well . . . for a while."
He says, "I'm so glad! I *know* I've been good."
I say, "I guess so, Tam—as good as you could."

When I dismiss the children and call it a day
Tam's desk is surrounded by popcorn and clay.
I don't understand it, but I love little Tam,
Though he is what he is, as I am what I am.

A TEARFUL RETIREMENT

I've been a teacher for thirty-five years.
I'm quitting now, but spare me your tears.
My back is deformed from the times I've been kicked.
My tongue is worn out from the boots I have licked.

I'm glad to quit and call it a day—
To throw in the towel and be on my way.
I hope certain members of the staff
Are able to wait till I clear out to laugh.

I've been under pressure and under fire
Till I feel an overinflated tire.
I'm all too familiar with teacher abuse,
Known only to those who have walked in my shoes.

Some co-workers give us a boost.
Others try to rule the roost.
If teaching isn't enough of a battle,
Add those who run to the office and tattle.

Most parents are helpful, dependable, too.
I treasure their friendships because they're true blue.
Some so appreciative seem to be,
But when the school term's over, they don't know me.

They want kids to learn and behave to a T,
But if I use the paddle, it's the gallows for me.
I'm cursed if I don't and slapped if I do.
I'm tired of the heat—want out of the stew.

A mommie will bring you her angelic prize
With the meanness gleaming from its beady eyes.
"I'm putting my darling in your care.
He'll give you no trouble anytime, anywhere.

"When you get to know him you will see—
My child is perfect, just like me."
Too long I've listened to this line of baloney
From parents who think I teach theirs and theirs only.

Through the years I've received note after note.
Been called everything but a billy goat
Mostly because I do not know
How to make a cardinal out of a crow.

One mom said my discipline needed improving.
Children shouldn't be talking or moving,
But just as soon as I lowered the boom
She moved little Junior out of my room.

I've thought of exchanging my desk for a bed.
Some kids come so sick, they can't hold up their heads,
Carrying a note and a bottle of pills,
Expecting the teacher to cure all ills.

If I don't give the pill at the time it should be,
A malpractice suit is in order for me.
If the child gets worse, I can't get a call through—
Mom's gone for the day—she had shopping to do.

I'll finally be taken off the list
Of those who are constantly shot at and missed,
And to those who pass judgement and criticize so:
I've forgot more than you'll ever know.

It's all yours, fellow teachers; I bid you adieu.
You have my best wishes—my sympathy, too.
Send me no flowers—no trophies, please.
I'll miss teaching school, like a dog misses fleas.

THE CARNIVAL

We had a fall carnival at our school,
To find out who was the biggest fool.
It was sponsored by the PTA.
When they want to make money, nothing stands in their way.

The biggest money-making thing,
Would be prince and princess, and queen and king.
The candidate that brought the most money in
Was the lucky one that would win, win, win!

When choosing a candidate, a teacher looked
For empty heads and full pocketbooks.
Soon the school was turned into trick or treat.
Teaching and learning took a back seat.

My little girl ran for queen this year,
So I got myself into high gear.
I sold everything I could find,
From roofing nails to blackberry wine.

I fixed junk food and popped popcorn
To sell at school in the early morn.
Soon the classroom and the halls
Were covered with Kool-aid and popcorn balls.

A kid would sell a cupcake to you,
After he'd licked it a time or two.
Chances on everything were for sale.
Cakewalks were held every day without fail.

Janitors ran with brooms and mops handy,
To clean up pop and melted candy.
Kids splashed and splattered all over the place.
The bigger the splash, the hotter the race.

People threw money every which way,
Including their savings for a rainy day.
I've spent every nickel I could find loose.
The light company's even cut off my juice.

I've done everything I could to make money.
Even robbed the bees, and sold their honey.
I wrote a bad check—I may go to the pen,
But what does it matter, as long as I win?

The big night finally did arrive.
The whole town seemed to be working alive.
Parents were milling 'round and 'bout,
While teachers worked till their tongues hung out.

There was high anticipation for the crowning.
Parents and grandparents stood around frowning.
Some wouldn't speak, they were so uptight.
Others had their fists cocked, ready to fight.

Many were ready to blow their lids.
It was open season on little kids.
As the time for the big event drew near,
The crowd neared the site, eager to hear.

The announcement was made. It was my Jan Cloy!
I'd put her over! Oh what joy!
I was envied by all. I was on cloud nine!
I treasured this moment—it was all mine.

How could I stand such ecstasy?
I pinched myself to make sure it was me.
Who would ever have thought that I
Could achieve an honor so very high?

Cameras clicked, and flash cubes popped.
I thought I'd surely blow my top!
She got a foil crown, and a five dollar bill,
Plus a trophy to set on the window sill.

I was elated! How I did smile!
(Though I'd eat brown beans for a long, long while.)
The tale was told—the die was cast.
I was the biggest fool at last.

A SHIP OF FOOLS

Welcome aboard the ship of fools.
The sign above the door says, "School."
Come on in and you will see
What education has come to be.

If you hear a loud scream, don't be alarmed.
It's probably just a broken arm.
Watch your step and you won't be
Our next unlucky casualty.

The principal says, "Don't come to me.
The supreme court took my authority."
Teachers aren't allowed to use a paddle,
Regardless of how many kids get addled.

Some dish it out—others take it.
If a kid can't fight, he'll never make it.
Students knock, push, and shout.
They call that "letting it all hang out."

There goes that shattered glass again!
—Another broken window pane.
If that same student breaks another,
Someone may threaten to call his mother.

The three R's have a new ID.
They're 'rasslin', rebellin', and robbery.
In school, we now have self expression.
It takes the place of learning lessons.

Down the hall comes Mrs. Peeve,
Complaining loud about sick leave.
She wants to know who left and why.
She will make sure no one gets by

Without a written note to her,
Telling how, why, when, and where,
She'll stir, until things boil and bubble.
She sparks her day by causing trouble.

Your ears will pick up Mrs. Wise.
She did not get enough supplies.
Although her shelves will hold no more,
She's inventoried on each floor.

One teacher got an extra pin
And two more sheets of onion skin.
Mrs. Wise will have her share.
She will make sure that all is fair.

Down two doors is Mrs. Glass.
She tries to teach while students sass.
She will retire by and by.
Meanwhile she'll laugh, so she won't cry.

It seems to be your lucky day.
A committee is here from the P.T.A.
The president gets up and shows
A ring for every teacher's nose.

Parents ring the 'phone all day
To see that things are run their way.
The secretary has many chores to fulfill,
Like cleaning noses and giving pills.

When it's dismissal time at three-o-five
Teachers are thankful to be alive.
They've pulled one more day of misery
With the help of strong coffee and tylenol-three.

I hope your tour has enlightened you
As to what modern education can do.
When you take discipline out of the schools,
You end up with a ship of fools.

TIME FOR SCHOOL TO END

I think it is time for school to go out.
Confusion and stress are all about.
Teachers have completely lost control.
Students won't even answer the roll.

Teachers are darting here and there,
Dodging books as they sail through the air.
Kids are using their pencils as spears,
Trying to pierce each other's ears.

Bus drivers wish they'd never been born.
They get eight or ten strangled every morn.
Aides try to help teach the kids what to do,
But have ended up with their shins black and blue.

The cooks fix food to please every whim.
The kids pick it up and throw it at them.
The janitor runs with a mop and a broom.
Kids see who can have the messiest room.

Substitute teachers say, "Don't call me.
I can't put up with such misery."
The art teacher's had to leave on the run.
All the kids will draw is a loaded gun.

The music teacher has ended his song.
Kids broke his piano playing King Kong.
A class has attacked the phys. ed. teacher.
She climbed on the roof, so they couldn't reach her.

The secretary's lost her composure, too.
She's been kicked around like a worn-out shoe.
She's stayed very late to get her work done.
Does she get any thank you's? No, not one.

The principal left, holding his head,
Went to the doctor, then took to his bed.
Come to our rescue, someone who has pull!
Pull a few strings and turn out school.

FIRST GRADE STUDENT

I'm a student in grade one,
But I am not having fun.
I sometimes wish I hadn't passed
Last year's kindergarten class.

I have a noisy, pushy teacher.
She yells louder than a preacher.
She's in a hurry—she won't explain.
She tells it once and not again.

She has no time for teaching sounds.
We go through books in leaps and bounds.
We work, study, memorize,
Until there's spots before our eyes.

I have to learn to multiply
Before September passes by.
Long division I must know,
Before November winds do blow.

Spelling words are long and many,
Like "archaeologist" and "Mussolini."
I hope, this week, I spell them all,
Or Teach will put me in the hall.

It's recess, but I am not through.
I don't work fast, as others do.
I'm working while my classmates play—
I am not having a very good day.

I wonder when I'll get to "use it."
If I ask permission, she may refuse it.
If I soon don't get a break,
Around my seat will be a lake.

I finish my work as playtime ends.
I wish I could have played with friends.
Now it's time to get going again,
But I take time to speak to Ben.

The teacher says, "I heard you speak.
No phys. ed. for you, this week."
I'd like to answer, but I'm too smart.
If I talk back, she'll say, "No art!"

I have much homework, I can see.
A long assignment for Mom and me.
We work until she starts to cry,
"You can't do it—neither can I."

If Mom and I can make it till spring,
We should know about everything.
If I learn all that's shoved at me,
I should be finished with grade three.

THE PREACHER'S WIFE

When I married a Methodist peacher,
I thought I'd landed a heavenly creature.
My husband was perfect—a dream come true.
Deeds of question he would not do.

A preacher's salary is quite small,
But I didn't mind at all.
I skimped and saved every dime
To see that our bills were paid on time.

I never missed his presentations.
He was devoted to his congregation.
He did all church work with pride,
And I was always by his side.

After we had children I was confined.
He went alone, but didn't mind.
He was busy every night,
Encouraging sinners to do right.

One night the neighbors kept our brood.
They said a break would do me good.
I went to the church to surprise my man,
But the only car there was widow Lynn's van.

I wondered where the members were.
It was prayer meeting night—they should be here.
Joe got home at twelve forty-eight.
A business meeting had kept him late.

I pretended to swallow his usual line,
But was learning the truth of this husband of mine.
The next night he said he would meet with the youth—
I followed, knowing I'd learn the truth.

Lynn was waiting at the church in her van.
She jumped in our car and took off with my man.
I felt my adrenaline begin to flow—
I saw how far I could trust Preacher Joe.

I laid down the law and set the preacher right.
No more meetings late at night.
I know now that a preacher will stray,
If a buxom female wants to play.

I see that things don't get out of hand—
'Though my husband's a preacher, he's still a man,
And no man is perfect in this life;
You can take it from a preacher's wife.

THE HAIRDRESSER

I'm a hairdresser. I try to please.
I snip, shave, and cut—I curl, twist, and tease.
You'd never believe what I go through,
All for the sake of a nice hairdo.

Mrs. Larkspur is an hour late,
Is very impatient—says she can't wait,
Wants me to stop working on Mrs. Howe,
And fix *her* hair, right here and now.

Mrs. Walls has three hyper girls.
They plunder and search and climb like squirrels.
They make a disaster out of my shop,
But not the first time does she tell them to stop.

Lennie Mae comes in with her hair all whacked.
It looks like a train's run over the back.
She looks like a lawn mower's cut her bangs,
And the sides look like she's sprouting wings.

She wants me to straighten up the mess—
It isn't easy, but I do my best.
She screams until her face turns blue,
And says, "You've ruined me! I'll sue you!"

Ms. Lamb comes in and says, "Do me up right.
I'm going to a fancy banquet tonight."
I give her the works—it takes trouble and time.
She writes me a check, but it's not worth a dime.

Next comes long-tongued Mrs. Bell
With gossip to spread and lies to tell.
She talks about young, old, big, and small.
She slights no one, but lies on us all.

Samantha wanted her hair dyed red.
I colored it exactly the shade she said.
She looked in the mirror and gave a few cries,
Then passed out cold, right before my eyes.

Mrs. Bear comes in with tote bag in hand,
Ready to steal anything that she can.
I try to watch, but when I turn around,
She takes everything that's not nailed down.

When the day is over, I'm ready to drop,
But still I have to clean my shop.
I can't help but feel that somewhere out there,
There's an easier job than fixing hair.

THE SECRETARY

I'm a secretary—my name is Ann.
I work for a prominent businessman.
I do everything but wax the floors,
In my slave quarters behind closed doors.

I'm trained to type and take dictation
And file away classified information.
But I work many hours and don't get paid
For running errands and playing housemaid.

I come to work at the crack of dawn,
To have doughnuts ready and coffee on,
Then I do paper work for the wife, Mrs. Ned,
Till my fingers cramp and my eyes are red.

Next I rush to the restaurant down the street
To get something for the boss to eat.
He sends no money for the tip.
If I don't pay it, I look like a drip.

There's a list waiting on my desk for me—
Phone calls to make, and people to see.
Mrs. Ned is so busy, she just can't do it.
I spend two more hours getting halfway through it.

Mr. Ned needs something from the grocery store,
So I have to go out and do errands some more.
When I return, it's getting late—
My secretary work has had to wait.

Ned dictates letters for me to do.
It's time to close the office when he gets through.
He leaves on the dot—his day is done,
But my letter writing has just begun.

He says to me, "Sorry you have to stay.
You should do your work early in the day."
He gets his coat and grabs his hat,
Leaving clothes I'm to take to the laundromat.

I'm hard at my typing till half past eight,
While any plans I've made have to wait.
I take this abuse from this sarcastic jerk—
If I stand my grounds, I'm out of work.

I keep late hours, and work like a fool,
Expecting anytime to grow ears like a mule.
If I can make it till Secretary's Day,
I may be rewarded a bale of hay.

THE WIDOW

I'm a widow—my name is Nell Ann.
I've lived ten years without a man.
Many people have asked me why
I've not found a man, as the years have gone by.

You'd better save your sympathy.
You probably need it more than me.
For twenty years, I was married to Ben.
Let me tell you the difference between now and then.

I can go where I please, anywhere, anytime,
And I'm not treated like I've done a crime.
If I take a trip to a nearby town,
Nobody's waiting with a scowl and a frown.

I can talk all I want on the telephone,
Without being told to leave it alone.
If I want to visit some of my kin,
I don't have to get permission from Ben.

If I don't want to scrub and clean,
Nobody's going to treat me mean.
If I make a flop of something I cook,
I don't have to worry about dirty looks.

If I like a program on TV,
Nobody switches the channel on me.
I can sit up and sew till my eyes turn red,
And nobody yells: "Come to bed!"

If I take a little drive in the car,
No one checks the mileage to see how far.
If I hit something and have a flat,
I don't have to face a nerve-wracking spat.

If I work overtime and come home late,
I'm not accused of having a date.
If I want to go on a shopping spree.
I don't have to take the third degree.

If I want to change wallpaper or paint,
Nobody's going to tell me I can't.
I can plant flowers beside my walk,
Without a lot of negative talk.

If I make plans, and they turn out bad,
I don't have to take any sass from Dad.
If I misread a road map and get turned around,
Nobody's waiting to put me down.

If I want to have a dog or a cat,
It won't have to dodge a baseball bat.
I'm free to go to football games,
Without being called a string of bad names.

Don't worry 'bout your man, I won't take him from you.
I've learned *plenty*, after all I've been through.
Now that you've learned about my single life,
Would *you* go back to being a wife?

THE DOCTOR

I am Doctor Anderson Little.
I help sick people in a hospital
By spending time prescribing pills
And helping folks overcome their ills.

Mrs. Lake's sugar is just too much.
I tell her, "Give up confections, and such."
She looks at me, as her eyes fill with tears,
And says, "I haven't had sweets for years."

When she gets her pen from her handbag I see
Oodles of candy—she's lying to me.
She rushes out to get medication,
Useless without cooperation.

Mrs. Cartwell is pregnant, again.
She weighs a hefty two hundred and ten.
I say, "Get your weight down. It's *so* bad for you."
She says, "Sorry, Doctor, that's too hard to do."

Mr. Jell's blood pressure's 'way too high.
I say, "Get it down, man! Mr. Jell, you could die!
For mercy sakes, let up on the salt!"
He says, "If I die, it'll be your fault."

Mrs. James comes in with a screaming tot.
He yells, "Doctor, don't give me a shot!"
I say, "The doctor is here to help."
He bites my arm and leaves a big welt.

Grandpa Smith has been fighting again.
This time I'll have to stitch his chin.
I say, "Mr. Smith, don't continue to fight."
He says, "I'll quit, next Saturday night."

Mr. Clark had surgery on his toe.
I look at it and say, "Oh, no!"
He says, "My stitches were too tight.
I cut them loose, the other night."

I say, "Wounds need tight stitches to close."
He says, "Well, Doc, that's how it goes.
I still don't want my stitches tight.
This time I hope you sew it right."

I have to do surgery on Mr. Hex.
He says, "If I have it, can I have sex?"
I say, "It won't hurt your virility."
He says, "That's all that matters to me."

Mr. Bow comes in, gasping for breath.
I say, "Cigarettes have caused many deaths."
He says, "Smoking, I don't regret.
I've smoked twenty years, and they ain't hurt me yet."

Claude comes in all shaky and white.
He says, "I quit drinking late last night.
I need help. My head's throbbing and sore."
Then he heads down the street to the whiskey store.

Mrs. Green comes in, acting quite lame.
She says, "I'm no better . . . my leg's the same."
There's malfunction—the fire alarm sounds.
She races to the exit like a big greyhound.

I work all day—it's a losing battle.
Sometimes I'd rather be punching cattle.
I feel like checking upstairs to see
If a hospital bed's left over for me.

MS. TONGUE

My name is Ms. Tongue. I live alone.
I spend much time on the telephone.
I talk from dawn till late at night,
Stirring up trouble and causing fights.

I had a man, but he headed south.
He said he couldn't stand my mouth.
I constantly keep an uproar going.
Seeds of evil I am sowing.

The couple next door is having a fight.
I called her late the other night,
To tell her he has a roving eye.
He winked at my sister as she passed by.

Nellie is mad at Sue Ann Kurr.
I told about Sue keeping secrets from her.
Mandy isn't speaking to Rose.
I told her Rose said she had a big nose.

Amy is mad at Louise Slatt.
I told her Lou said that she was too fat.
Sandra is mad at Millie Cole.
I told her Millie said she stole.

If you have some gossip that you want spread,
Call me—I'll even get out of bed.
I tell and tattle from one to another.
I'd make up lies on my own mother.

WATCH—YOU MAY GET WHAT YOU PRAY FOR

I'd been very concerned of late.
I'd had no luck in finding a mate.
I was not getting younger—had no time to lose.
It was getting too late to pick and choose.

I had searched high and hunted low,
With no success—nothing to show.
I decided the thing to do was pray
For a prospective husband to come my way.

At a church picnic the third Sunday in June,
I met a man, named Malcom Boone.
"My prayers have been answered," I happily said.
"This must be the man I am meant to wed."

Malcom was bald and a little too fat,
But I said to myself, "I can handle that."
It wasn't very long till he asked me for my hand.
Soon I'd be wearing a gold wedding band.

We had a wedding in early fall,
With flowers, bridesmaids, ribbons, and all.
I planned a happy married life.
I would be the perfect wife.

For awhile, our marriage went so-so
Then Malcom said, "I want you to know
I'm the man of this house, and the man's in control.
You will do as I say. That's the woman's role."

This wasn't exactly what I had planned,
But we'd work it out, hand in hand.
Soon he was running things his way.
When he gave orders, I had to obey.

I had to rush home when my work day was done,
To cook and clean . . . I stayed on the run.
I wasn't allowed to keep in touch
With lifelong friends I enjoyed so much.

He wouldn't let me buy new clothes.
I went to work with runs in my hose.
He chose the programs we'd watch on TV.
We did as he said with no input from me.

I soon grew tired of this kind of life.
This wasn't my dream of being a wife.
If this was what married bliss was about,
It wasn't for me. I wanted out.

I decided the thing I should do was pray
For this miserable creature to go away.
Ere you pray for something, think hard about it.
Will you be better off with or without it?

When you have a good life and can do as you choose,
Don't get the crazy "man needing" blues.
I asked for a man. Now I regret it.
Watch what you pray for—you may get it.

MY MEANDERING LOVE LIFE

I'd been married ten years, when suddenly I
Decided to follow my roving eye.
I went looking and soon I found
Many girls willing to slip around.

I began to enjoy a romantic life,
—More fun than being home with my wife.
I told her my work was keeping me late,
And lived it up on date after date.

My wife stayed home, while I ran around
With different girls all over town.
After several months of this exhausting life,
I decided again to be true to my wife.

I left work early, expecting to see
My darling at home, waiting for me.
When I entered the house, no one was there.
I found this written on a note in my chair:

"I've relit a flame with an old beau of mine.
We're leaving today, on flight thirty-nine.
Some love lives run true, but others meander,
And what's fair for the goose, is fair for the gander."

LOVE CONQUERS ALL???

When I saw him, I knew that he
Was the only man for me.
His looks were far beyond compare—
Tall and dark, with wavy hair.

We began a courtship. I did all
The tricks I knew to make him fall.
I had to have him for my own.
I wanted him, and him alone.

It did not bother me that Jack
Was from the wrong side of the tracks.
My friend warned me to think it through.
I asked them: "Why? Our love is true."

I married Jack in early fall,
Sure that love would conquer all.
We moved into a homely shack,
But I was happy—I had Jack.

He found a decent job, at last.
I thought our money worries were past,
But he didn't work very long.
He said the boss had done him wrong.

I found out that my loving spouse
Was happy staying at the house.
He only lived from day to day—
From birth, he'd been brought up that way.

He didn't frown on poverty.
I had responsibility.
I worked two jobs to make a living.
He did the taking—I did the giving.

I couldn't buy anything new.
I barely paid bills, when they came due.
I looked around our shabby shack,
And decided I'd had it with handsome Jack.

This was not my kind of life.
I was a servant—not a wife.
I packed his clothes and bade him go
Back to the poverty he loved so.

I got my divorce in early fall.
True love does not conquer all.
When I look for a new heart throb,
I will make sure he has a job.

THE OTHER WOMAN

When I was a glowing twenty-three,
I saw a man that appealed to me.
I gave him the eye and he came my way,
So we sat and talked a big part of the day.

Tim was in his thirties—married, of course,
But planning shortly to get a divorce.
'Though he was married, his life was lonely.
His wife was interested in the kids, only.

We soon began a torrid affair.
I knew it was wrong, but I didn't care.
My best friend begged me to let him be.
I accused her of trying to take him from me.

Tim had no money to spend on me.
He had to support a family of three.
When we went on dates, I paid every cent,
Leaving barely enough for my rent.

I gave up all my social life,
To play second fiddle to this man's wife.
I felt it was worth it—I truly loved him.
My whole life was wrapped around Tim.

He promised that when his kids were grown,
He'd marry and have a life of our own,
That there was no closeness between him and his wife.
I was his one and only—the light of his life.

Tim said his wife had a shape like a bear,
A huge hooked nose, and stringy, dry hair.
Many nights I waited for him to 'phone,
For a few stolen moments to call him my own.

One day I decided to go and see
His ugly wife, and family.
I knocked on the door with a false I.D.,
And was shocked at the sight that I did see.

She had beautiful hair and was dressed just right.
Her face was pretty—her smile was bright.
Tim said they were married, only in name—
She was expecting a baby, just the same.

I got so mad, I fairly shook.
Through my stupid blindness, I had been took.
Here's some advice, and you'd better take it—
Give your heart to a married man and he'll break it.

Watch when you hear that pitiful plea:
"My wife doesn't understand me."
If a man asks you to pay for a date,
Cut him out of the picture, before it's too late.

If you ever play the waiting game,
It'll bring you heartache and a bad name.
Now when I get struck on a handsome man,
The first thing I look for is a wedding band.

I'd rather spend my remaining days single,
Than be the third corner of a love triangle.
Marriage is meant for two, not three—
The other woman I will not be.

ON A CHECK

I got a job. I worked five days.
Work is too much for what it pays.
Working hours start too soon,
And there is not a break till noon.

For lunch I furnished my own food.
I really thought the company should.
The workday did not end till four.
Work was nothing but a bore.

This would not do! No work for me.
Hard work and I do not agree.
I had to figure out a way
That I could loaf and rest all day.

I promptly started making plans—
Soon I would be an idle man.
With my kids and my mate,
I would be living off the state.

I let my hair and whiskers grow
And learned to hold my hip just so.
I learned to limp when I walked
And jerk my neck when I talked.

I wore my clothes as weeks passed by.
The odor almost reached the sky.
I put my toothbrush out of sight
And chewed tobacco day and night.

Things went on for quite some time.
I wore a glaze of grease and grime.
When I looked like a whippoorwill,
I was ready for the kill.

My wife led me to Doctor Trent.
The doctor did not like my scent.
He sent me on to Doctor Pink,
Who then sent me to see the shrink.

They checked to find out my IQ.
I made a score of thirty-two.
When all was done they made my day.
They signed me up on DPA!

Now I live a life of ease.
I sleep as late as I please,
And get my money without fail,
To buy such things as wine and ale.

Shrimp and t-bone I now eat.
Food stamps provide for me this treat,
Leaving plenty cash for me
For tickets for the lottery.

I'm owner of a brand new car.
I travel near—I travel far.
Folks frown at me, but what the heck?
I've got myself on a check.

POOR PEOPLE HAVE POOR WAYS

I got a job—the pay was good.
I'd live it up. I really should.
There were many things that I
Had yearned for, but just could not buy.

I wouldn't be like Uncle Hayes,
Who'd been conservative all of his days.
I told him money was to enjoy.
He said, "I'll tell you something, Boy.

I came up hard. I did without.
I know what need is all about.
Although my car is not so fine,
It gets me there, and it's all mine.

My modest home is mortgage free,
And plenty plush enough for me.
I've saved up for a rainy day.
If I need something, I can pay.

"I know my limits," said Uncle Hayes.
"Poor people have poor ways."
Uncle Hayes's philosophy
Didn't make a dent on me.

My income began to multiply,
So I started rolling high.
I bought myself a fine Corvette—
The most expensive I could get.

I went down to the shopping mall,
And bought new outfits—shoes and all.
Soon my money all ran out,
So I started charge accounts.

I felt that I should take a cruise.
The sea would take away the blues.
I went first class—I did it all,
But I was heading for a fall.

When I got home, I soon could see
Many bills awaiting me.
I knew that I'd gone overboard,
When I clashed with my landlord.

I'd had a blast—I'd lost my head.
Now I was thousands in the red.
I had no food—what would I do?
My power had been cut off, too.

The finance company took my car.
I hadn't got to drive it far.
I went to call on Uncle Hayes
And told him of my foolish ways.

I told my uncle I was broke.
This time I listened, when he spoke.
He said, "I will bail you out,
If you will take a different route.

Money's slow to come, but fast to go.
It's made to spend, but not to blow."
Now I agree with Uncle Hayes—
Poor people have poor ways.

MY WILL

I know that life is fleeting by
And realize it's time that I
Make my mind up what to do
And whom to will my fortune to.

First I started counting friends.
My relatives, I counted then.
I tried very hard to see
Favors they had done for me.

My list was soon so very small,
That I had next to none at all.
I thought of things they'd refused me,
And the many ways they'd used me.

Soon an awakening came to me.
A brighter light, I then could see.
Who'd worked hard for what I owned?
I'd worked my fingers to the bone.

My body's sound—my mind is, too.
There are some things I need to do.
I need to take a long vacation,
To see the beauty of our nation.

My car has far too many miles.
I need a bigger one, with style.
I'll get myself suitable clothes
To wear to concerts, plays, and shows.

After I tour the U.S.A.,
I'll board a ship and sail away
To see some sights across the sea,
Including Greece, and Italy.

Ere I am old and near the end,
My worldly fortune, I will spend.
I'll leave enough to pay my bills—
I will not need to make a will.

TV PREACHER

I'm a preacher on TV,
But I do not preach for free.
Give me money in big bills,
And don't forget me in your wills.

If your heart is filled with lust,
Hell fire will burn you to a crust,
Unless you send to me some loot,
To help me pay my prostitute.

I wear clothes of quality.
I'll let no one outdress me.
My wife wears the latest fashion.
Mink and diamonds are her passion.

On the stage, I stomp and rave.
You have a soul I want to save.
Let me rid you of your curse,
After you unzip your purse.

I drive costly, fancy cars.
I ride in style—to the bars.
It takes cash to operate.
Send money now—do not wait.

You widows have my sympathy.
You have a hard life, I agree.
Although your income is quite small,
Send it. I can use it all.

With money from the sick and old,
I bought a watch of solid gold.
Senior citizens are so good.
They send me checks and don't buy food.

I live in a palace grand.
There's none finer in the land.
You know my lifestyle isn't cheap.
Sow your cash, so I can reap.

I preach until the sweat does roll.
Brother, let me save your soul.
Don't let payday pass me by,
Or I will pucker up and cry.

If you don't help me with my costs,
My dear brother, you are lost.
You're bound for Hades, can't you see?
—But you won't get ahead of me.